The Silvertop fairies

A story of the mountains

Written by Tim Healey
Illustrated by Robert Broomfield

PUBLISHED BY THE READER'S DIGEST ASSOCIATION LIMITED

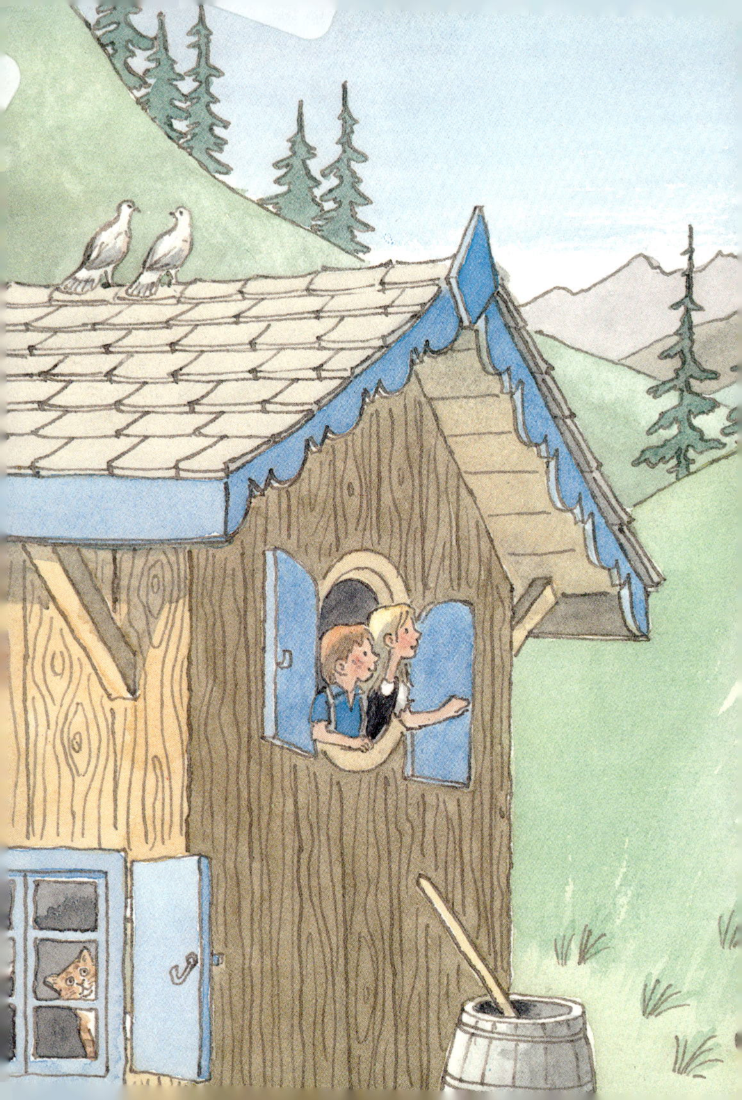

Ella and Peter were a poor woodcutter's children who lived in a high mountain valley. Their bedroom was an attic and through its little round window they could see the glistening peak of Silvertop Mountain.

Silvertop Mountain was famous. People said that it was the home of fairies who left silver coins under the pillows of sleeping children.

"I wish the Silvertop Fairies would visit us," said Ella one evening. "Then we could buy mother a new shawl, and father the new boots that he needs."

"Yes," replied Peter. "But are fairies real?"

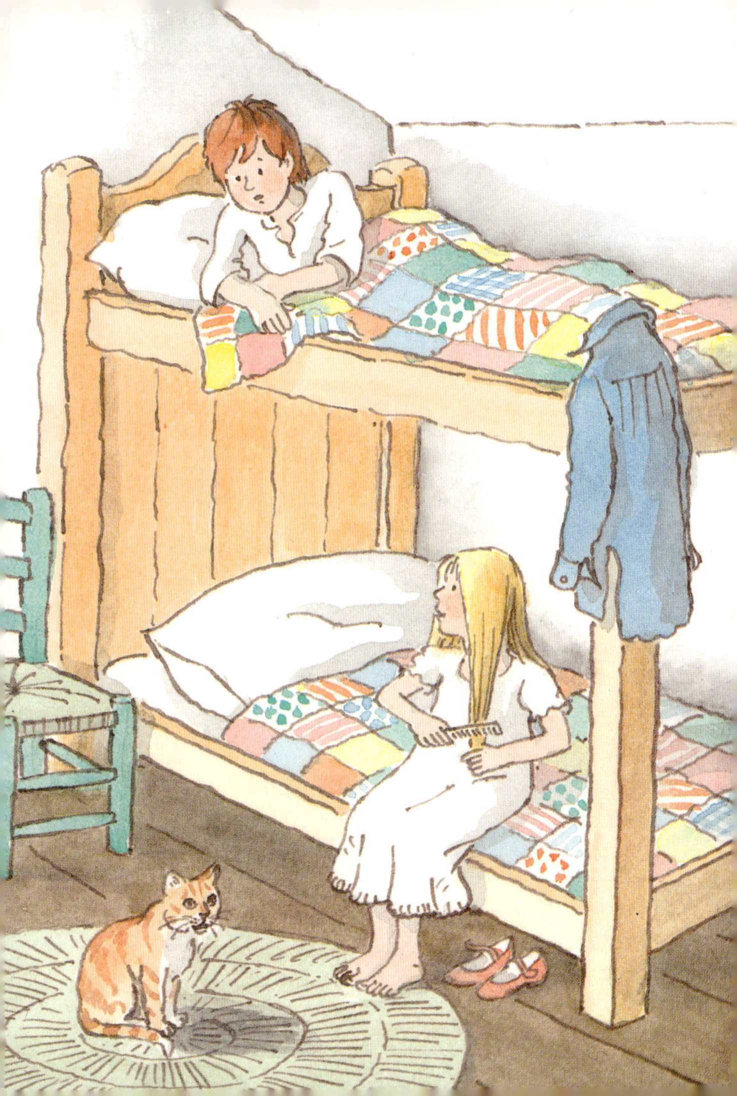

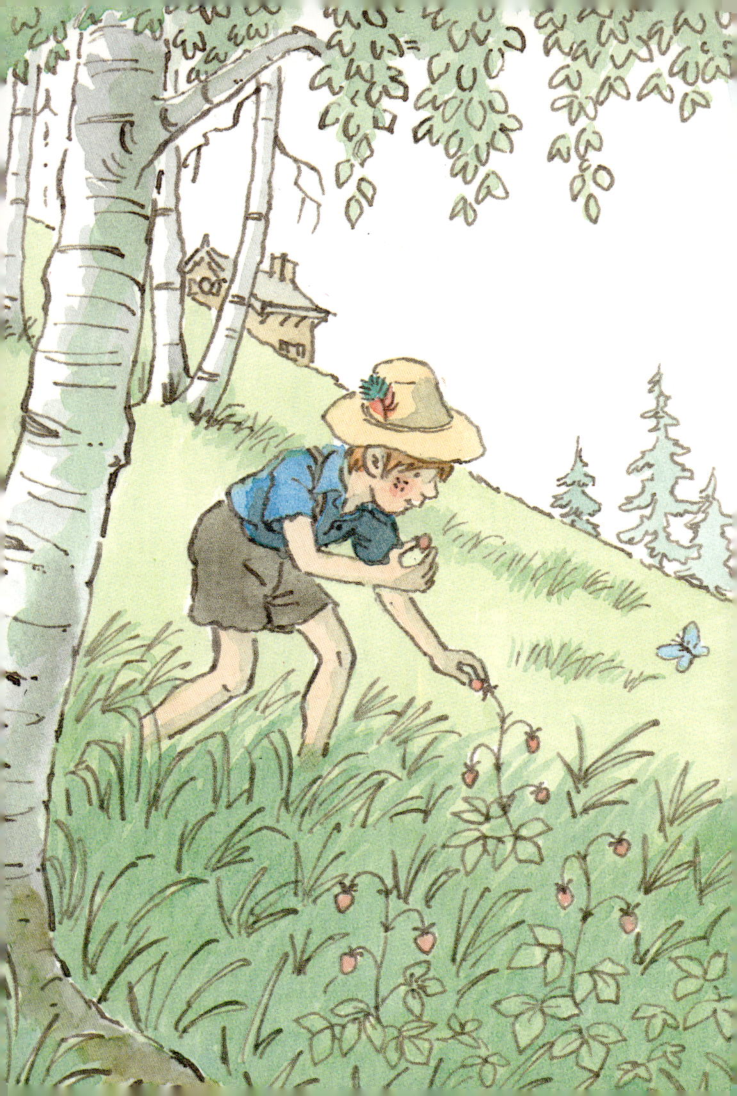

Next morning the children set out
to gather wild strawberries from
the woods and slopes of their valley.
They knew many shady places
where the plants grew.

And their path took them to the foot of Silvertop Mountain, where an old woman sat resting in the shade.

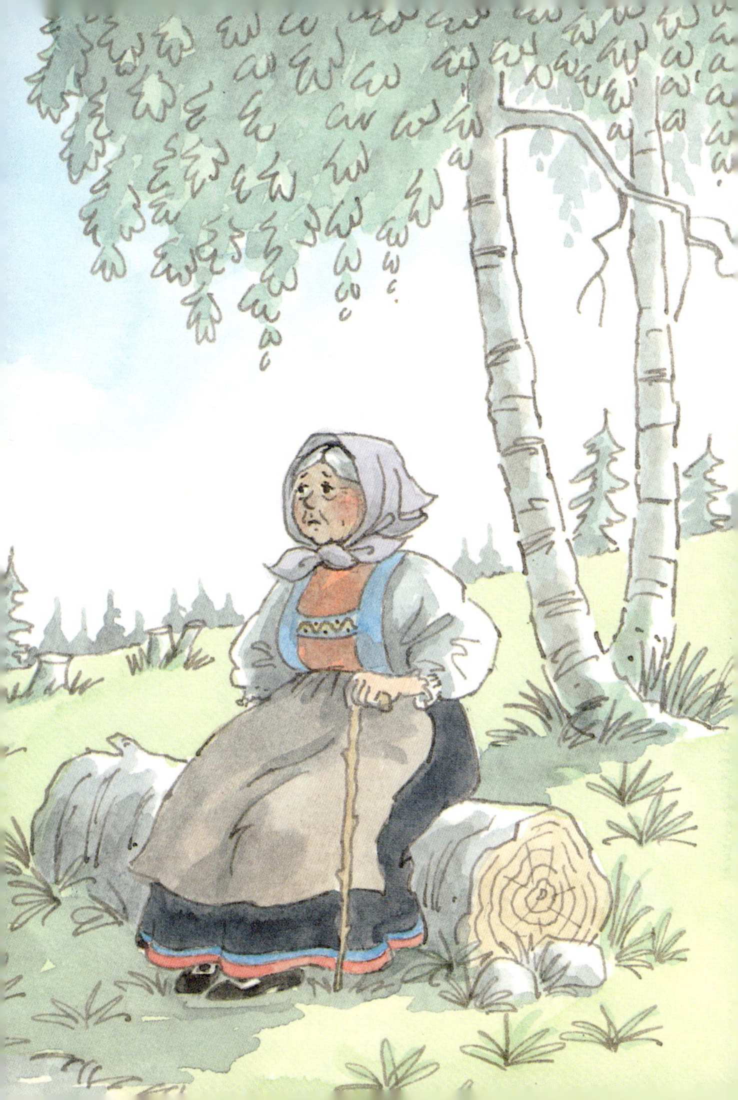

The old woman looked very tired. The children asked if they could help her, and she replied in a faint voice, "I am ill, children. I am ill from the heat. And there is only one thing that will cure me. I need summer snow to cool me down."

Summer snow? The children wondered where they could find such a thing. Then Ella remembered that there was snow at the peak of Silvertop Mountain. Up there, people said, it was so high and cold that the snow stayed all the year round.

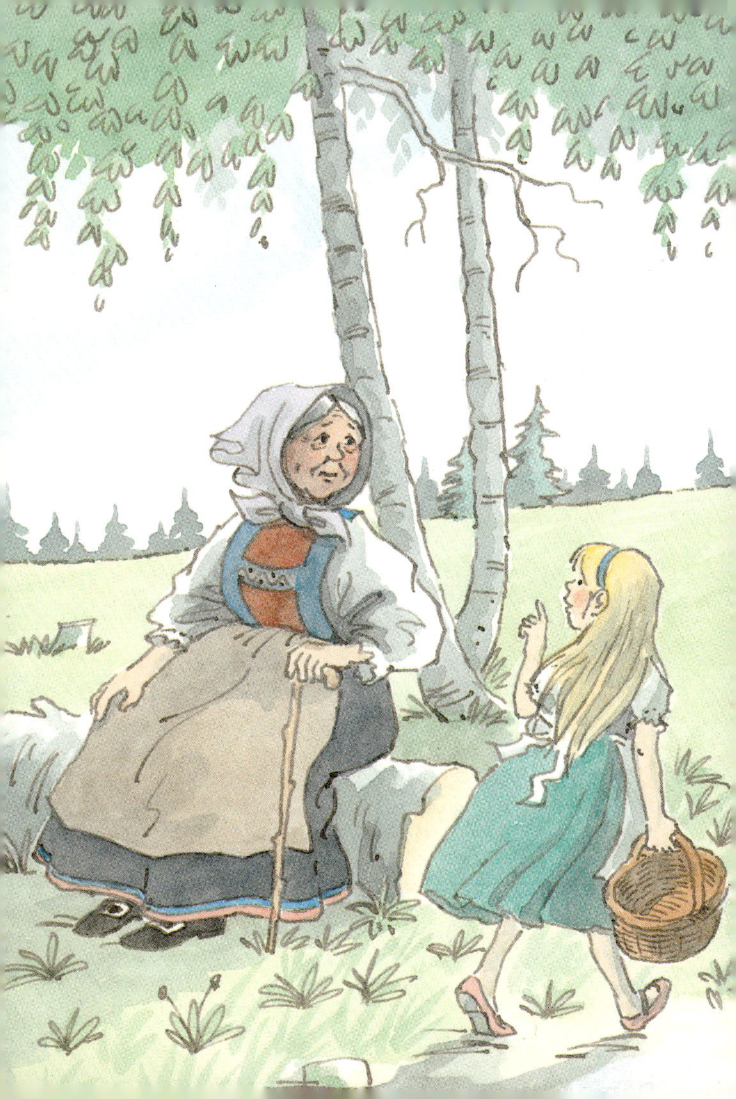

"We will bring you summer snow," said the children. And they set off to climb the mountain, following the rough track that led up.

The path took them through pinewoods where crimson crossbills fluttered among the trees. Ella and Peter went quietly, for they hoped to catch a glimpse of the Silvertop Fairies.

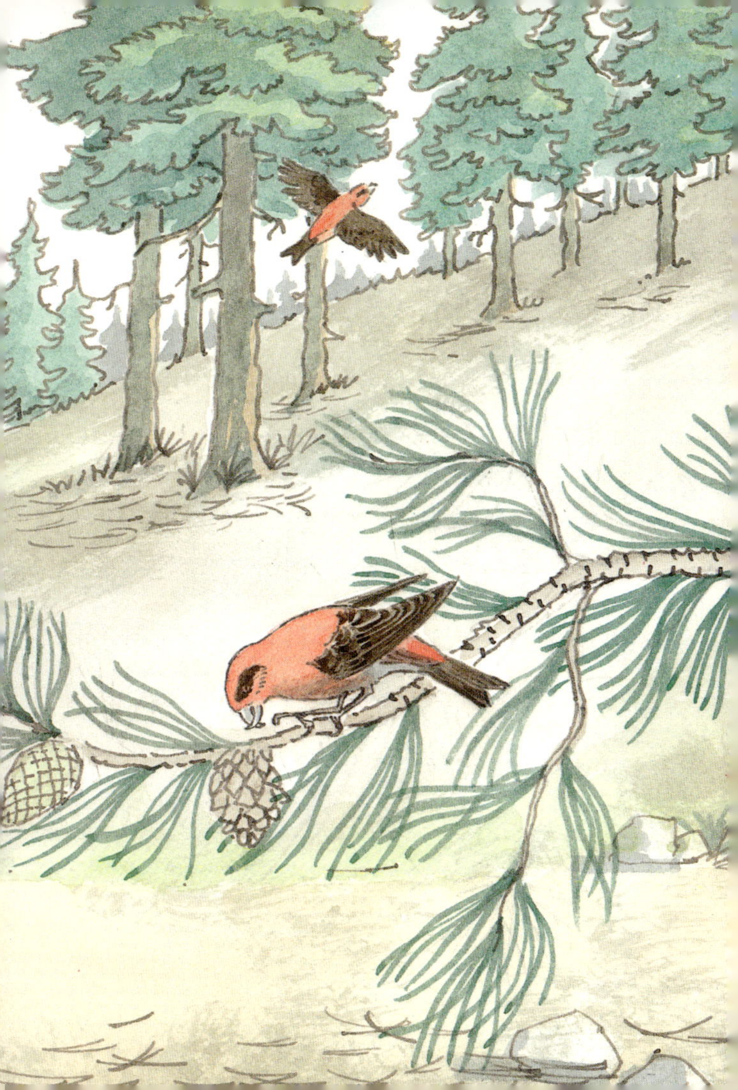

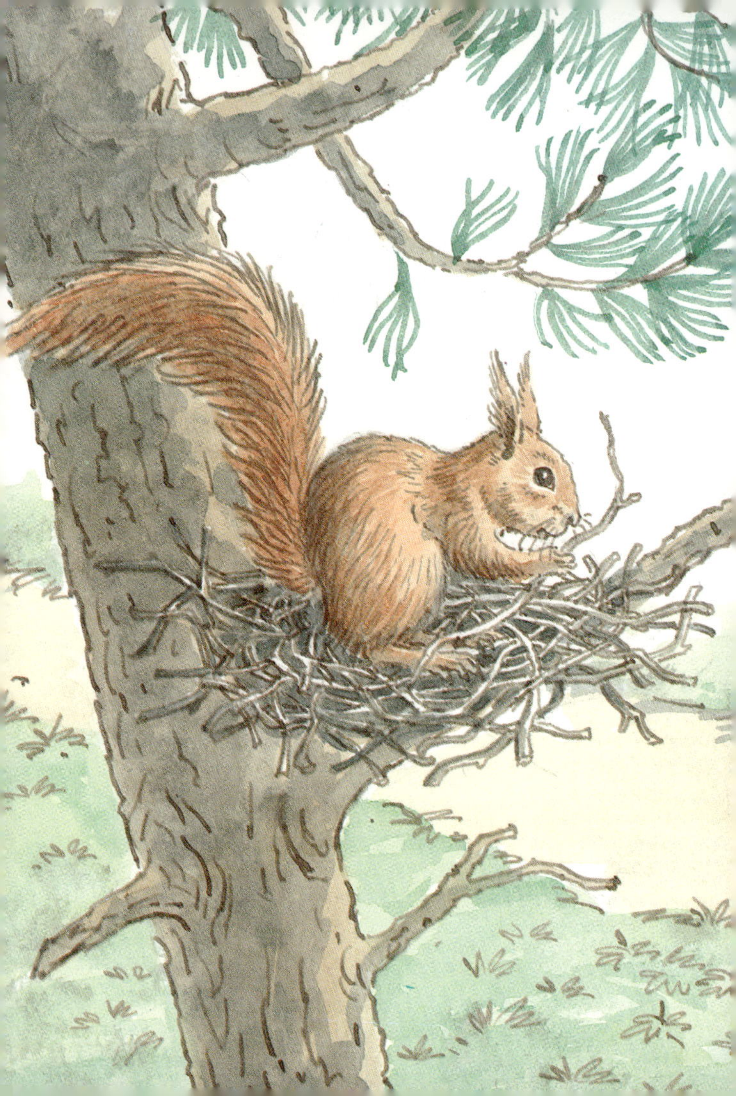

The children saw no fairies. But they did spy a red squirrel building a nest of twigs high in the branches of a pine.

Above the forest, the path led through high pastures. Cattle grazed there and the tinkling of their bells seemed to fill the air with music.

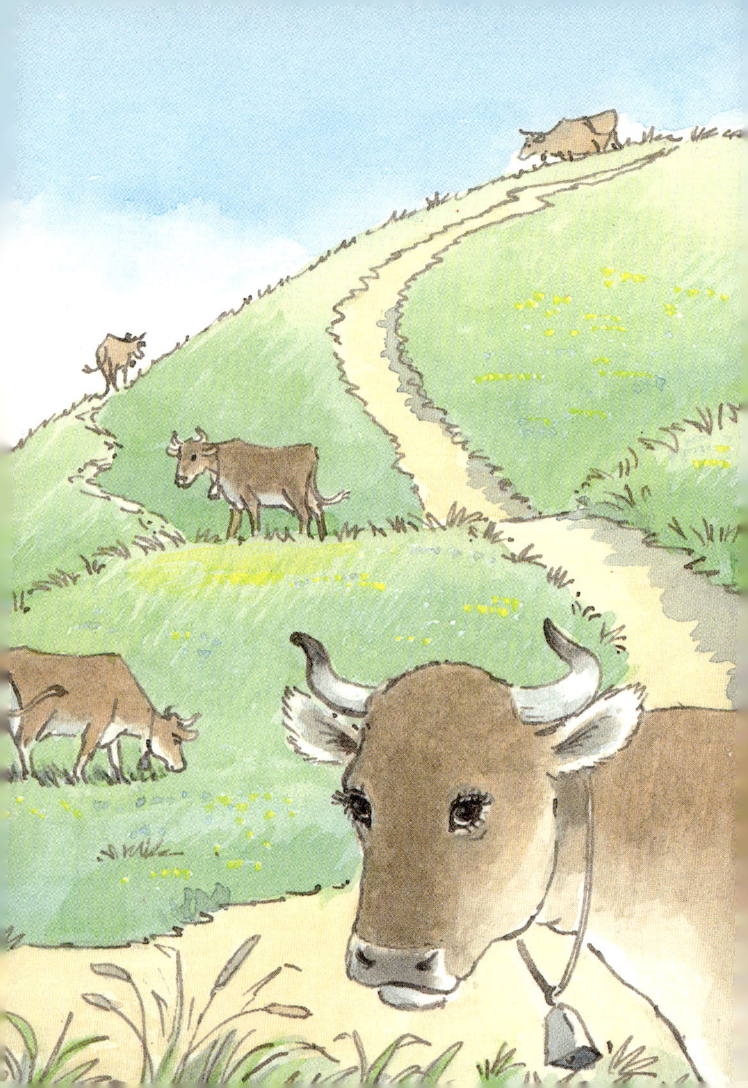

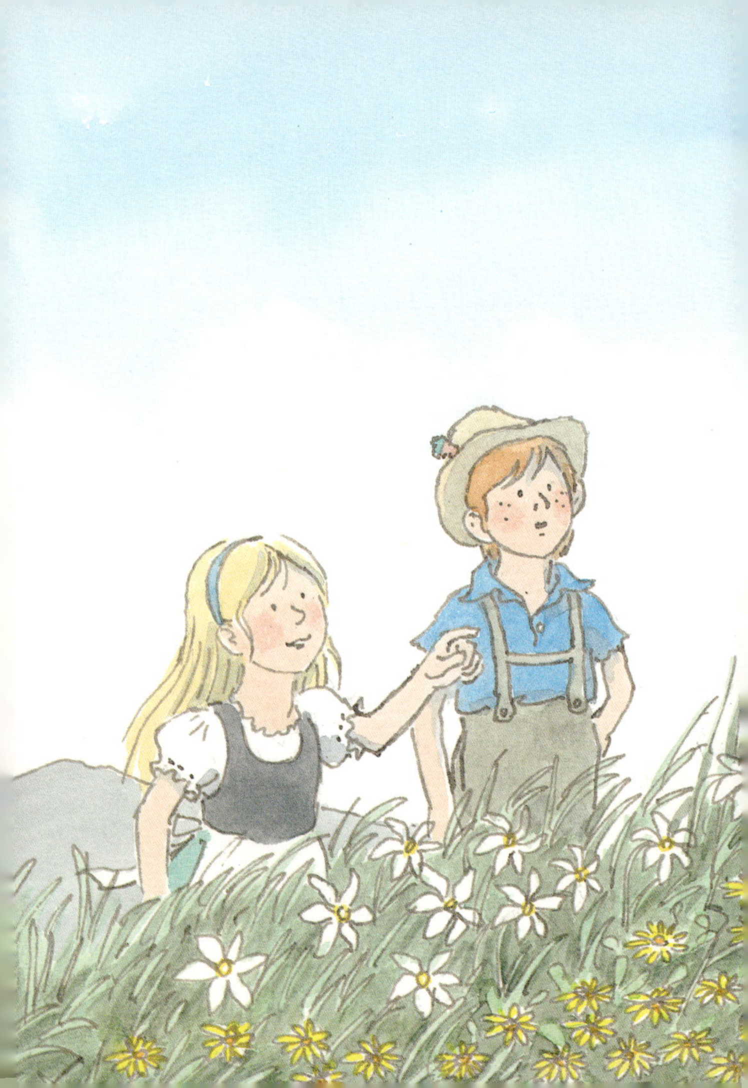

No fairies could be seen. But the pastures were dotted with lovely flowers. There were star-shaped flowers and trumpet flowers and flowers that burst like sunshine.

In places, the pastures shimmered with a thousand colours.

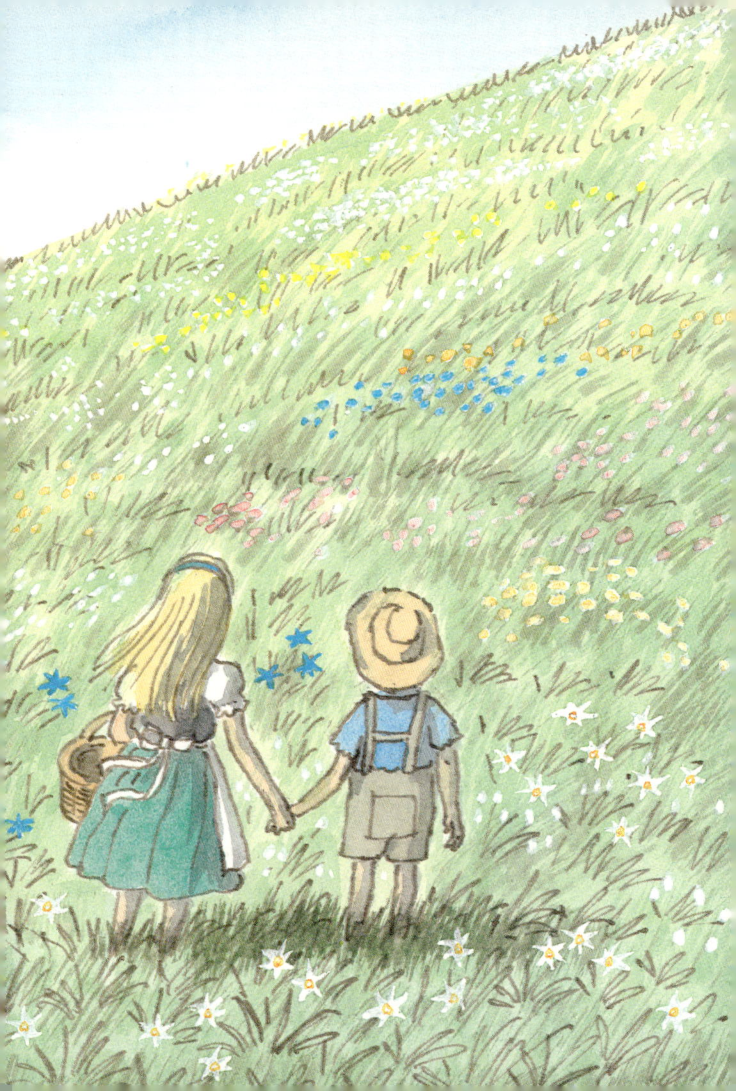

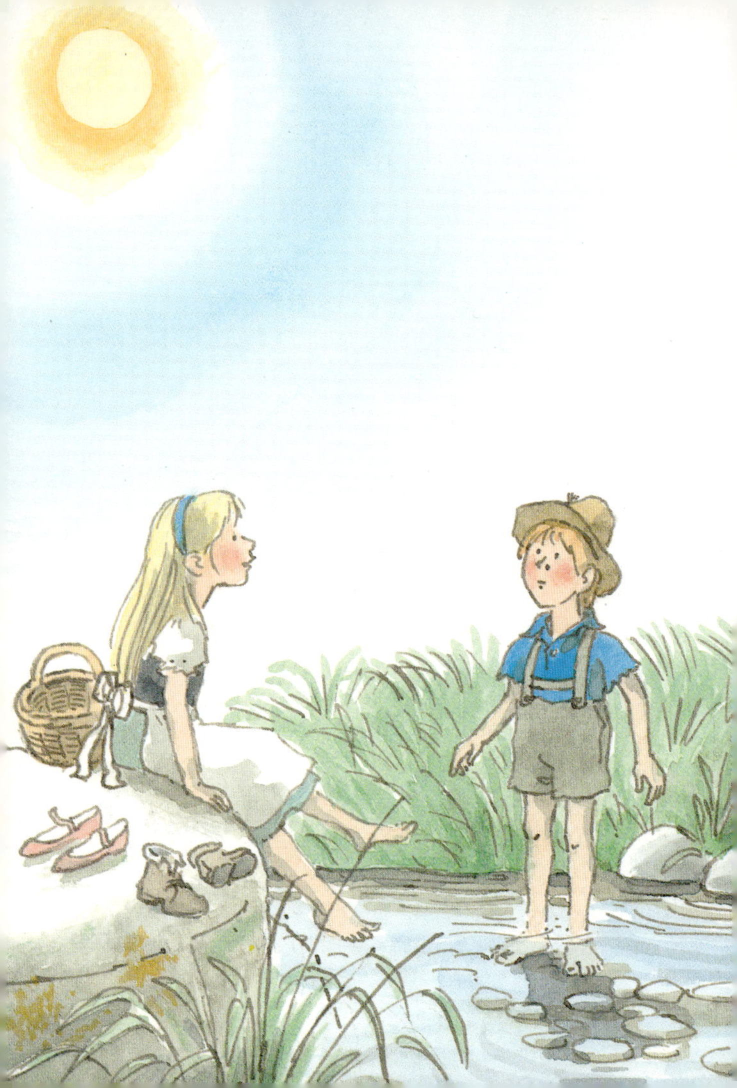

The children bathed their feet in a chilly mountain stream. "We must climb on, now," said Ella. "The old lady needs the summer snow and we have not found any yet."

And so they climbed onward. The track led steeply up through places where the grass grew thinner and thinner. Bare rocks loomed all around. Hardly any flowers grew; only a few shy blooms which peeped out between cracks here and there.

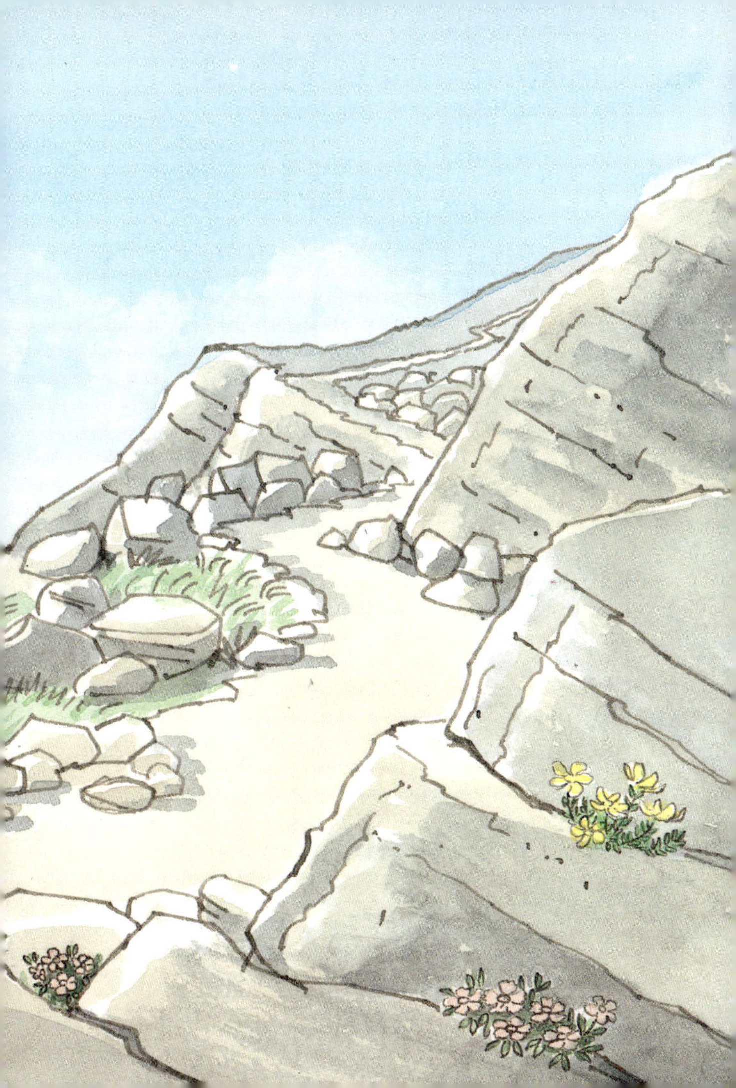

The children grew tired as they trudged on. And though the sky was still blue, they felt a great coldness in the air. "Will we ever reach the snows?" asked Peter, lagging behind. Before Ella could answer, she saw a shadow flit among the rocks up ahead. Was it a Silvertop Fairy?

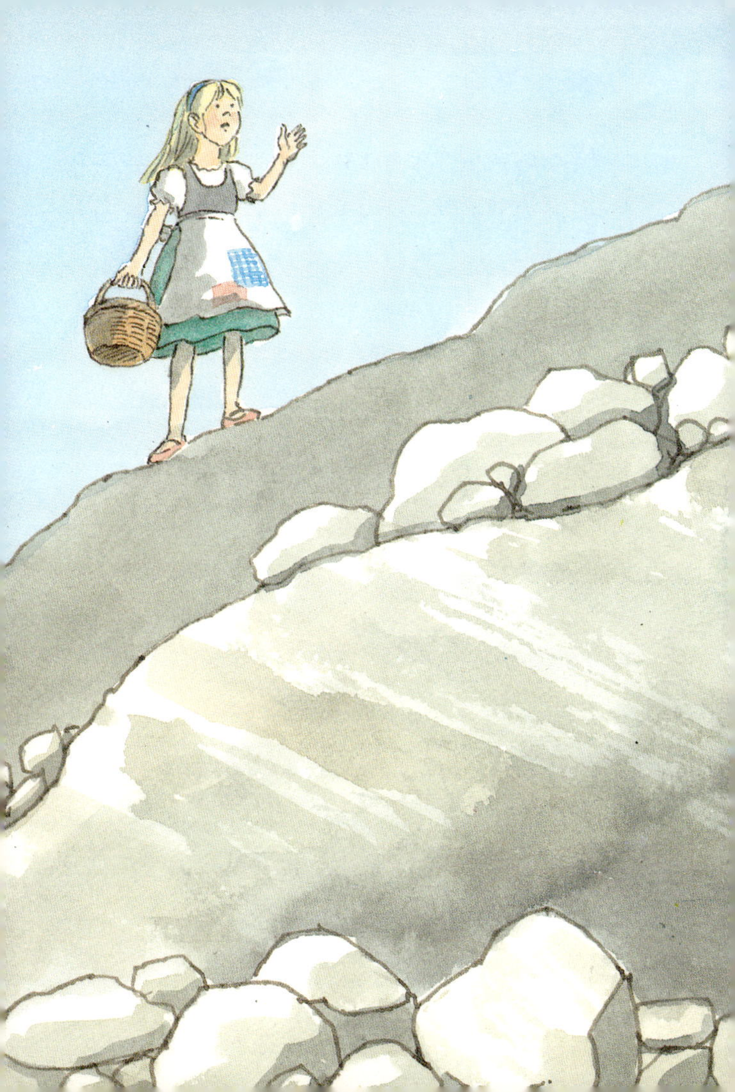

No. But it was a beautiful creature which looked like a small deer. It was a chamois.

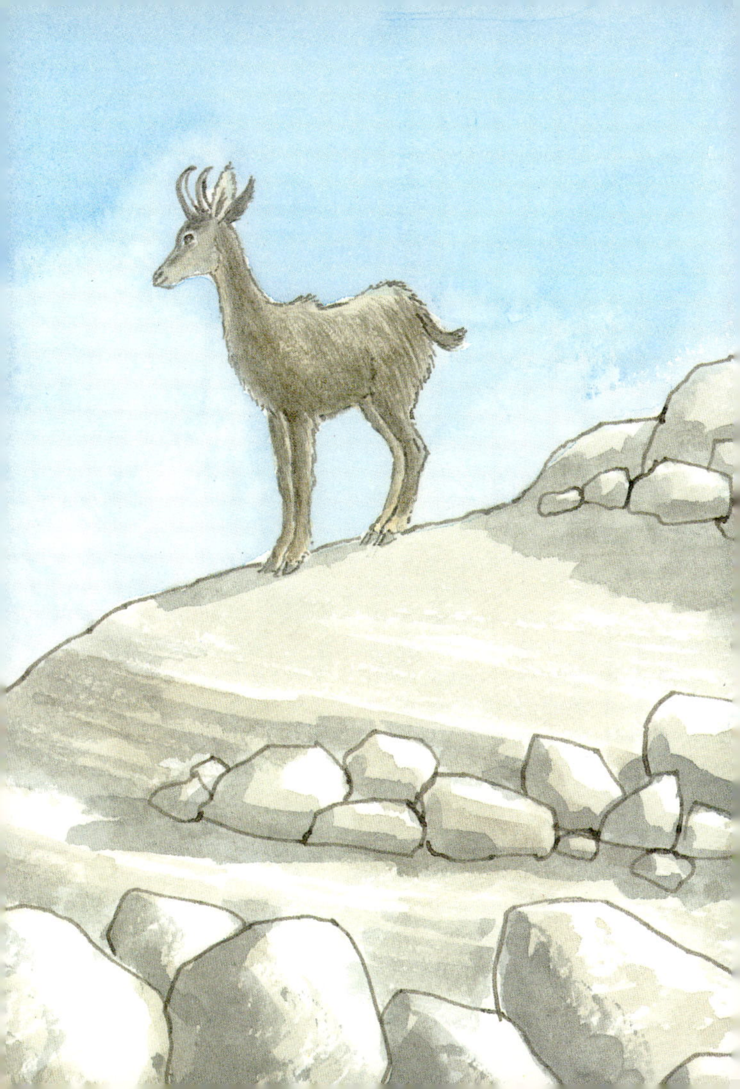

The chamois leapt gracefully over the brow ahead. The children hurried up the path after it. And as they came to the ridge they saw stretched out beyond sheets and sheets of dazzling whiteness. They had reached the snows at last.

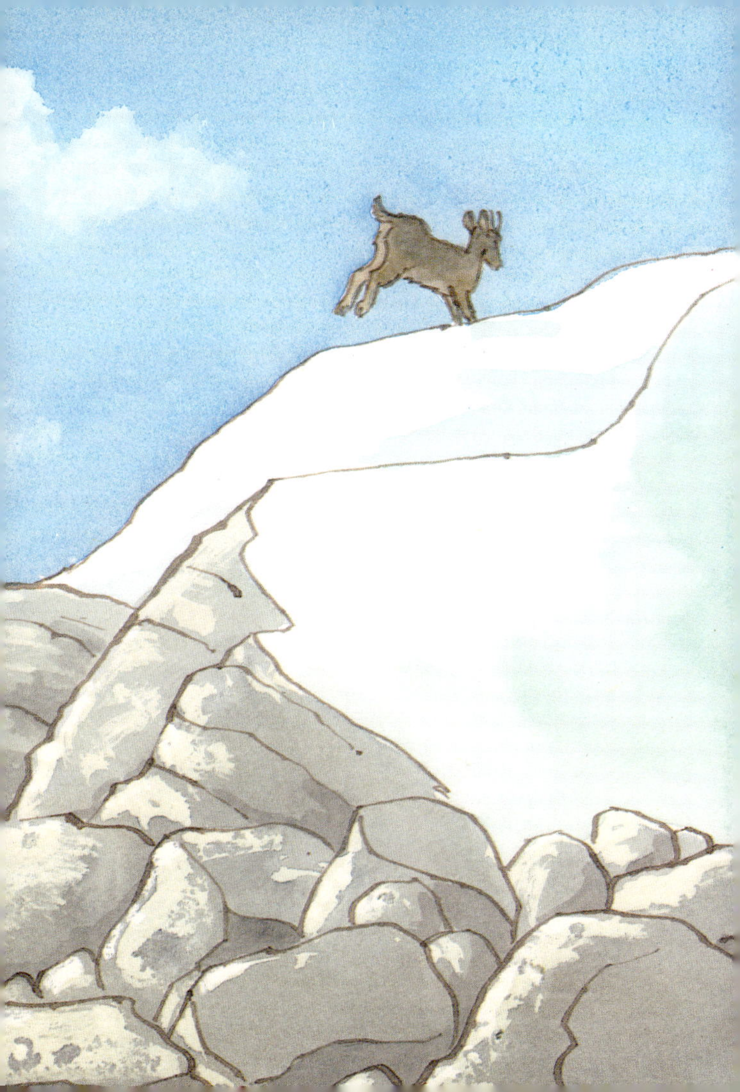

"Hooray!" chorused Ella and Peter. They ran to the snow's edge and danced there for joy.

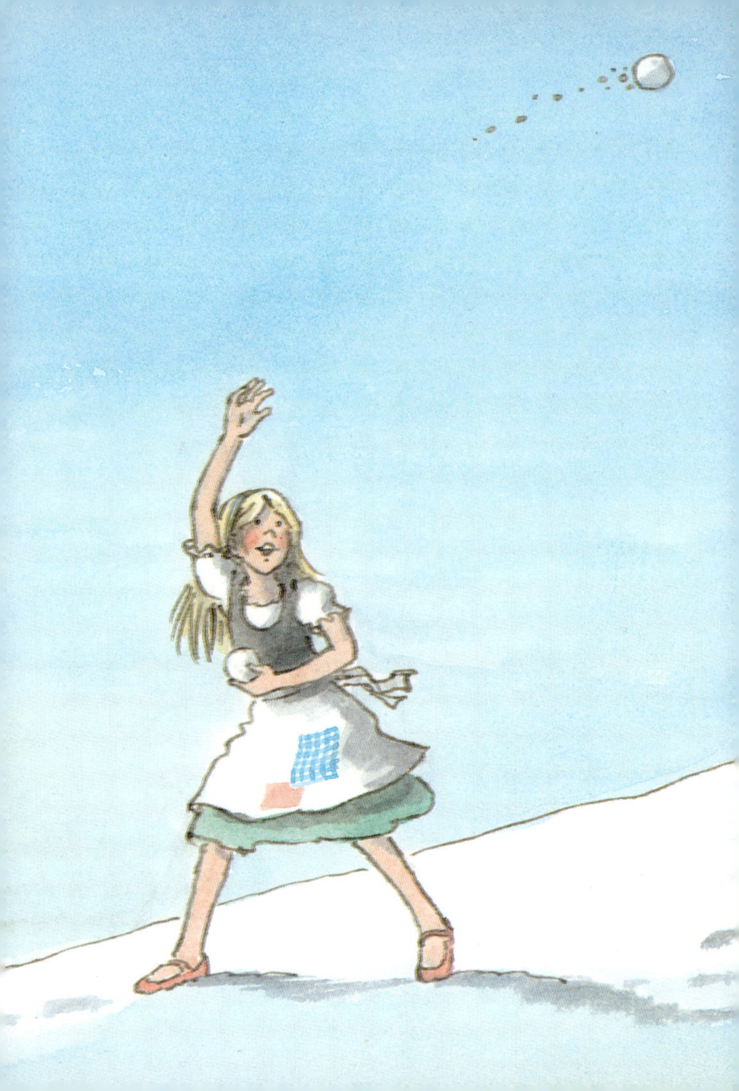

They made snowballs and tossed them at the vast blue sky.

Then they looked back down the path they had followed. Far, far below they could see their own green valley with its woods and fields and cottages.

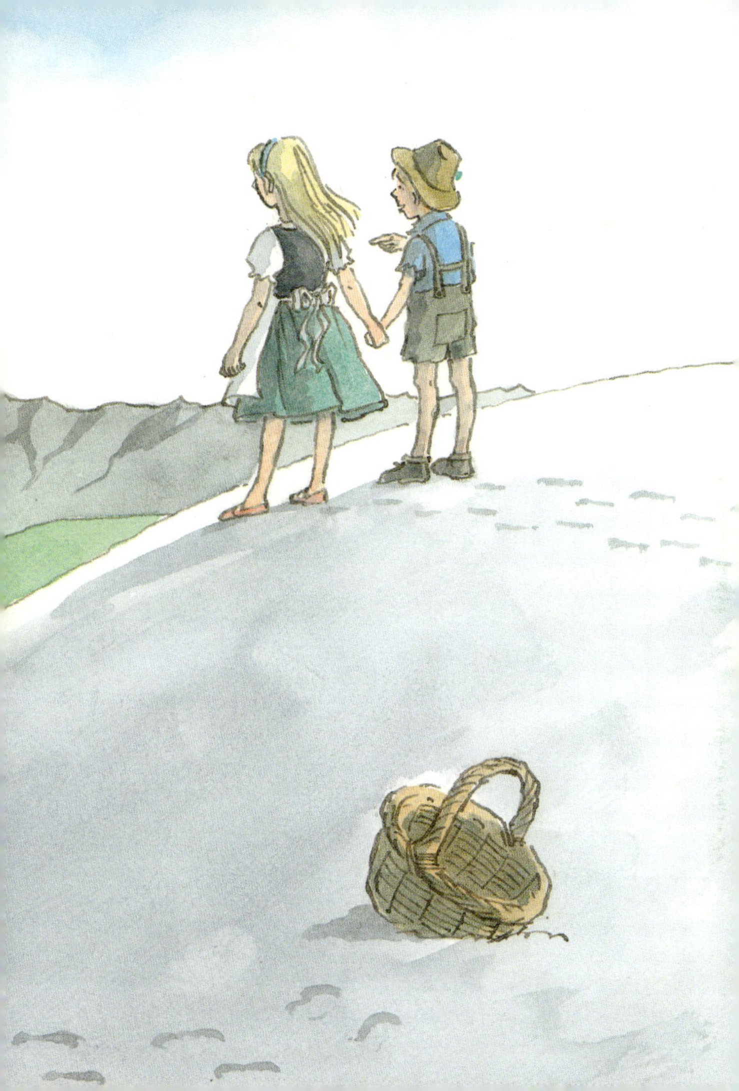

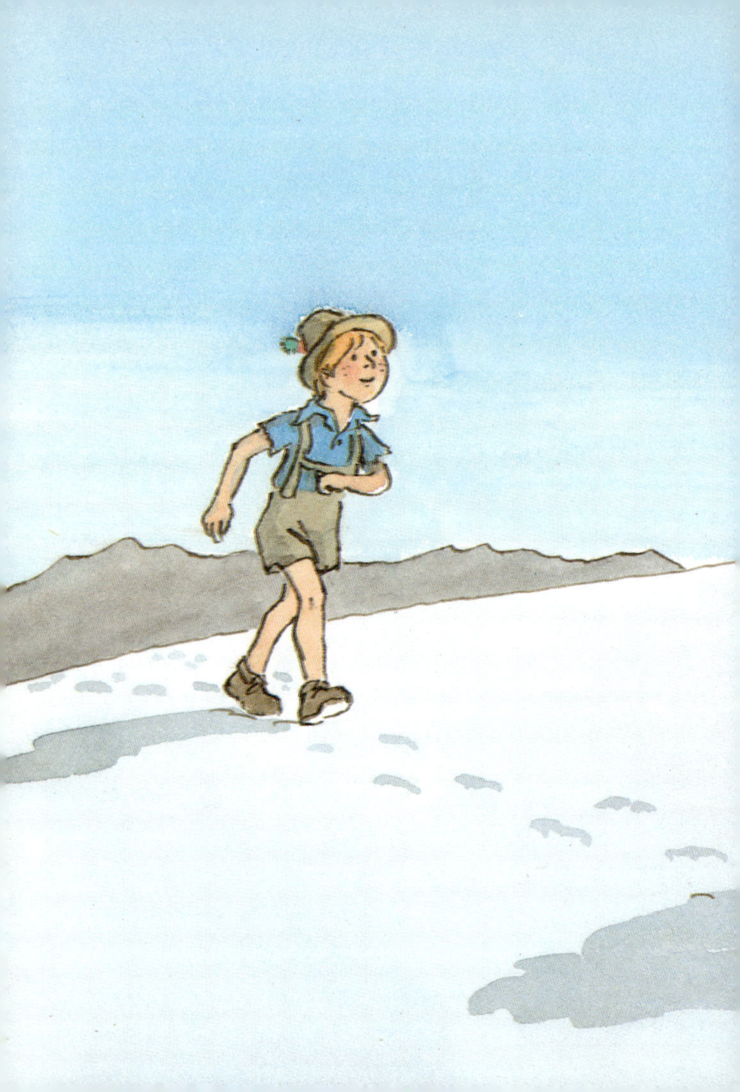

"We must hurry now," said Ella.
"Quick, fill the basket."

When they had piled the basket high with snow, the two children hurried back down the path. They came down much faster than they had gone up. It seemed that in no time at all they were back at the place where they had met the old woman.

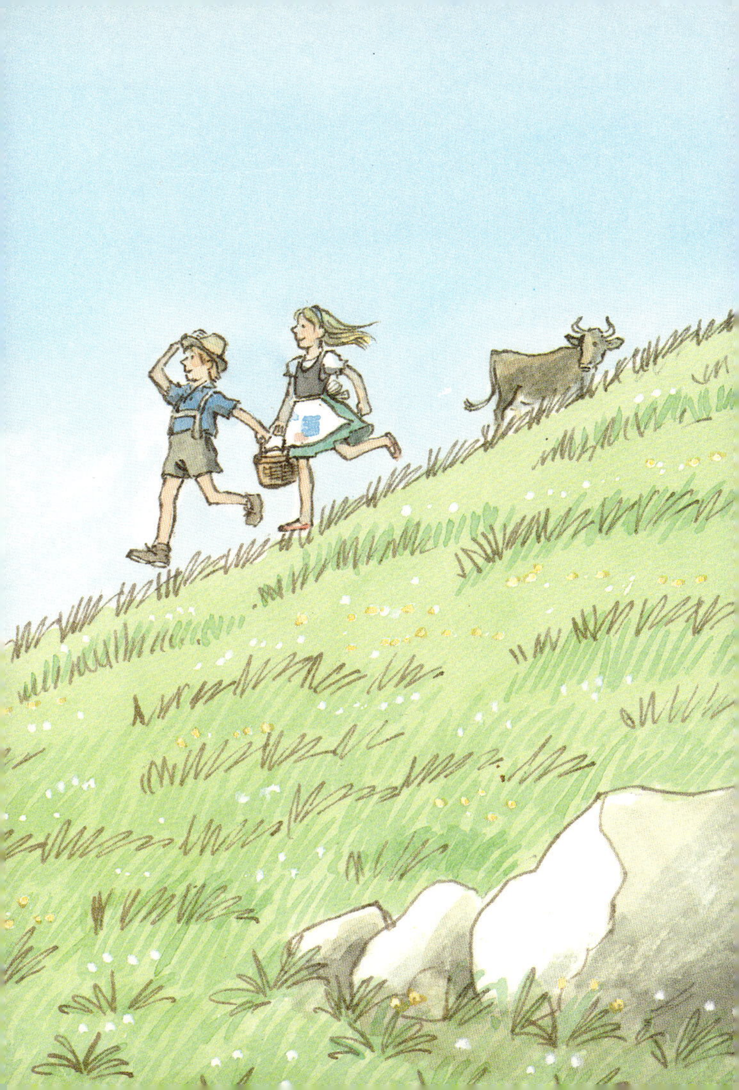

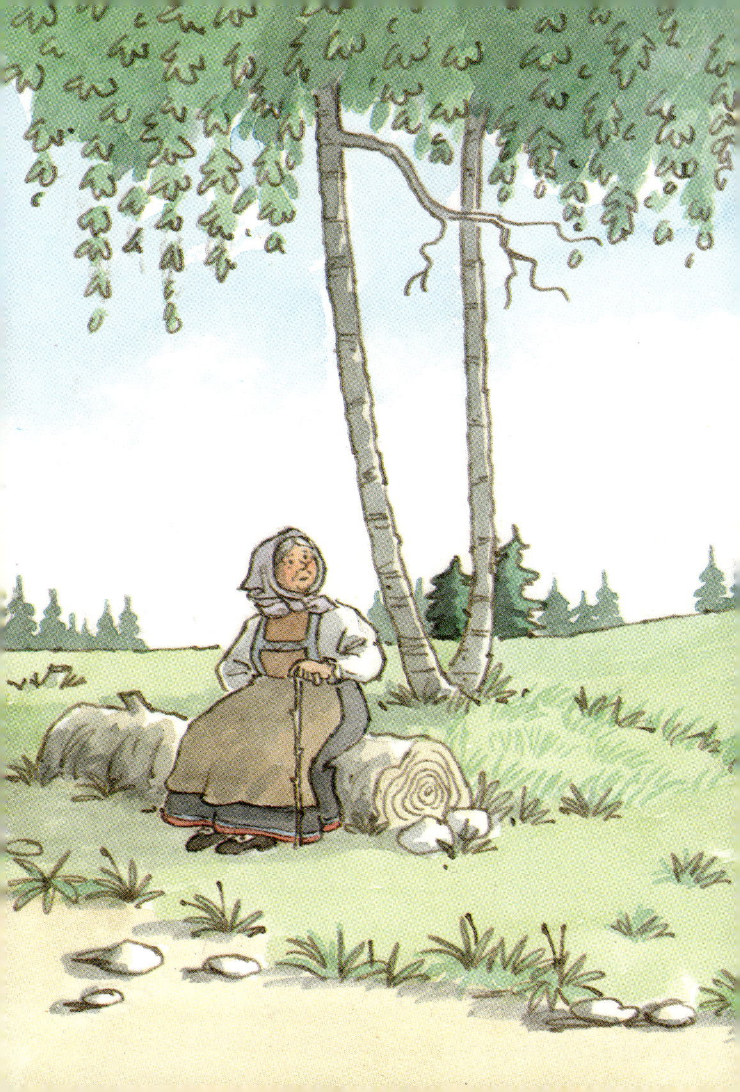

She was still sitting there when they arrived. The snow from the mountain top had started to melt in the warm air of the valley. But there was still plenty left in the basket.

The old woman smiled gratefully as they brought the snow to her. They described all the wonderful things they had seen on their adventure. "We even made summer snowballs!" Peter laughed.

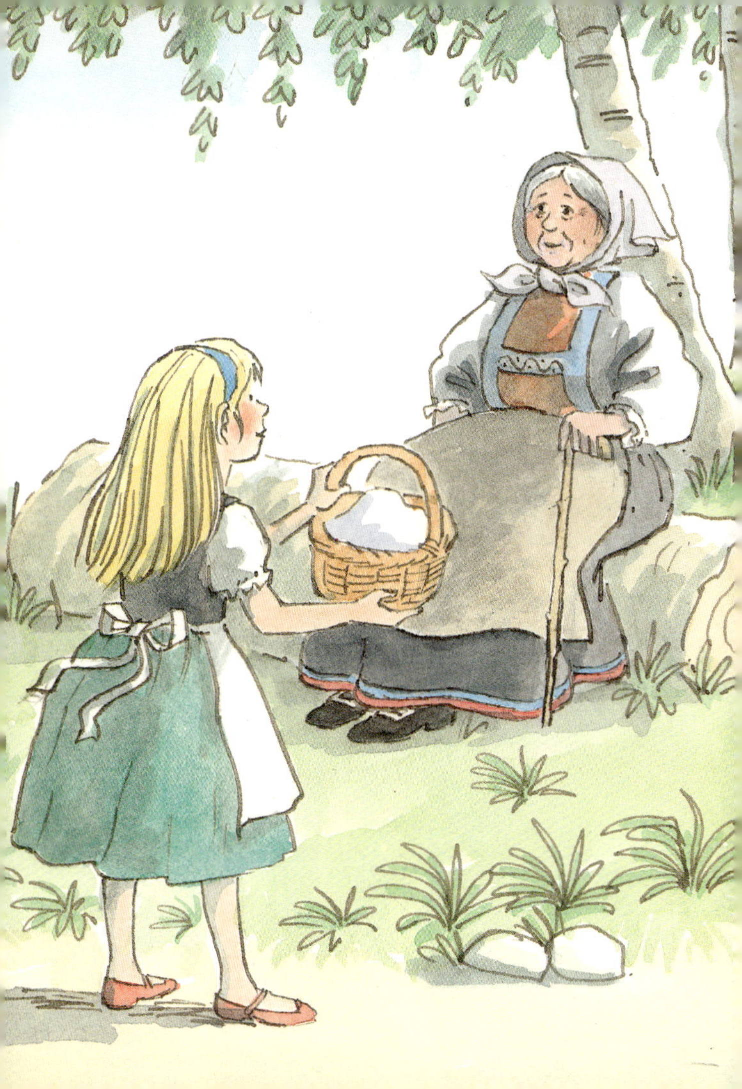

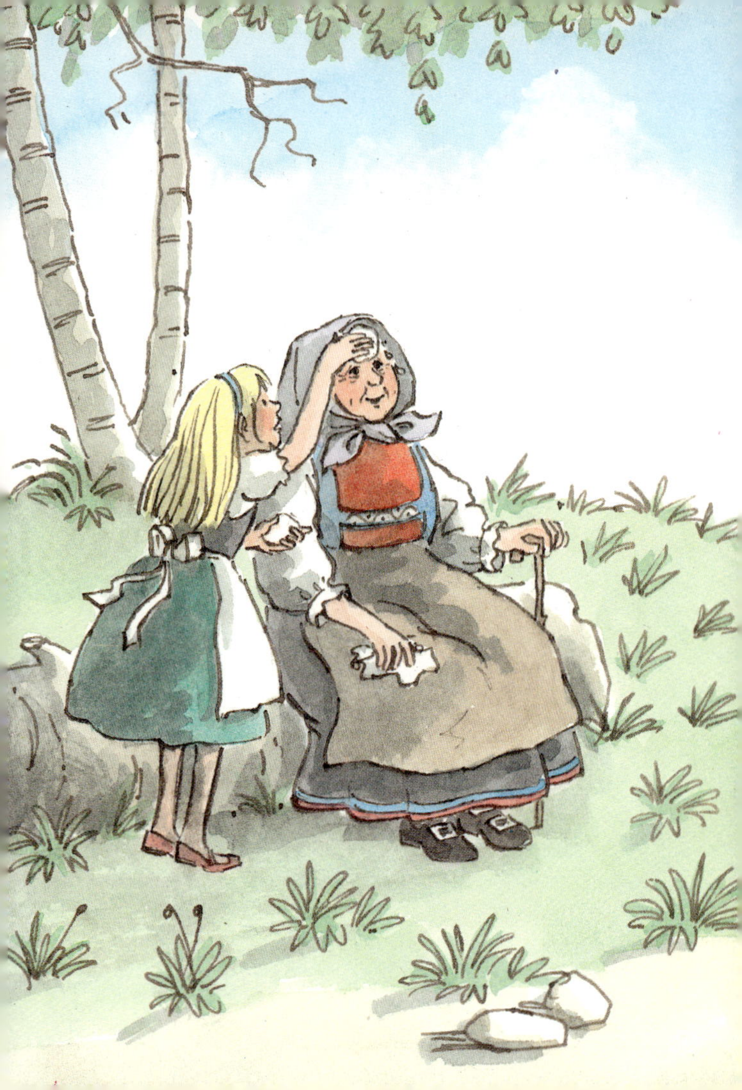

"And did you meet a Silvertop Fairy?" the old woman asked. "No," said the children, a little sadly. "We climbed right to the top of the mountain and didn't see a single one. So we don't believe in fairies now." And they mopped her hot brow with handfuls of snow.

As they did so, a strange thing happened. The old woman's wrinkles smoothed away.

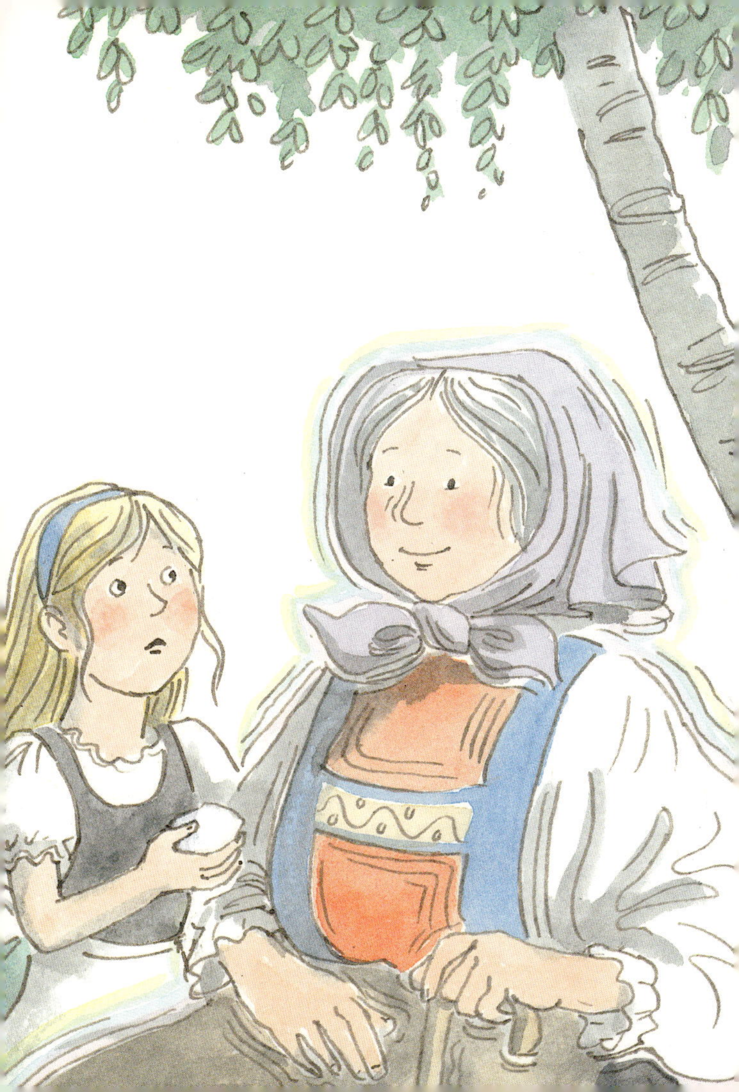

She became younger and younger, changing at last into a beautiful fairy princess.

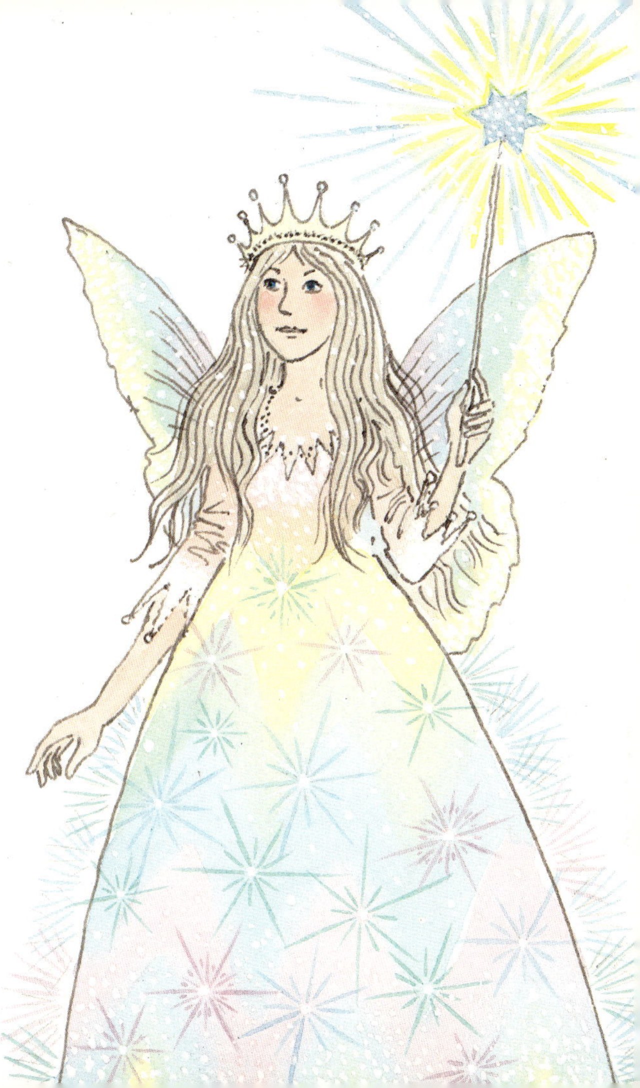

The fairy smiled one glowing smile, then vanished into thin air.

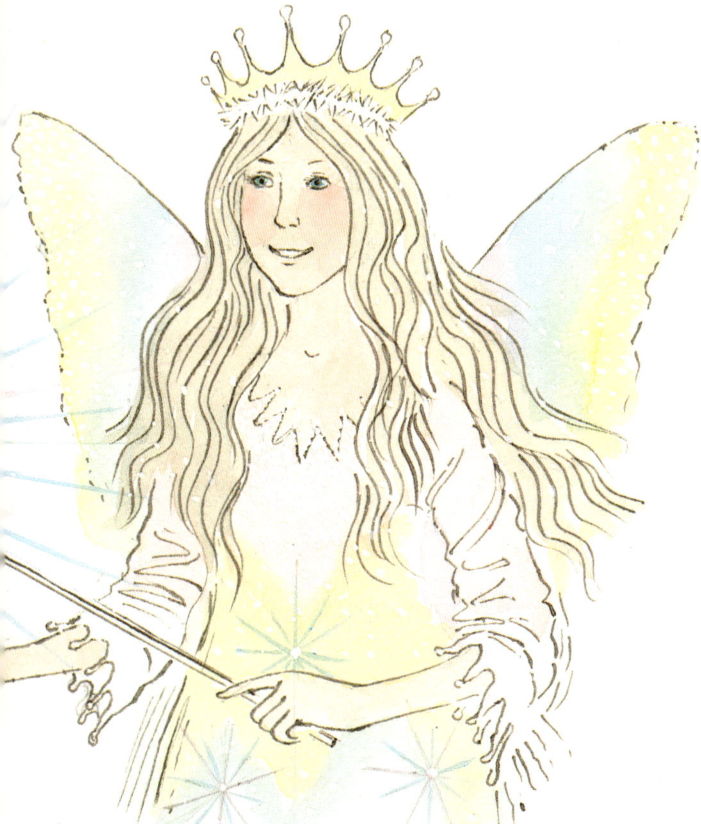

The children started back in wonder...

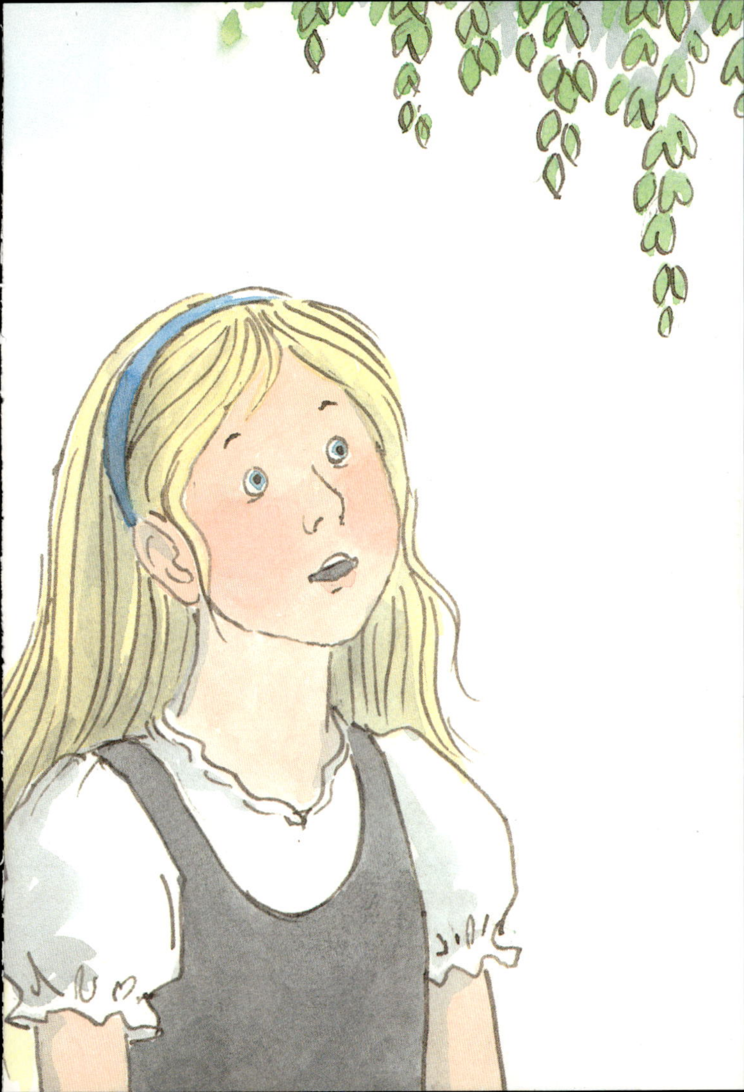

... and they found that the heap of snow in their basket had melted into a sparkling mass of silver coins!

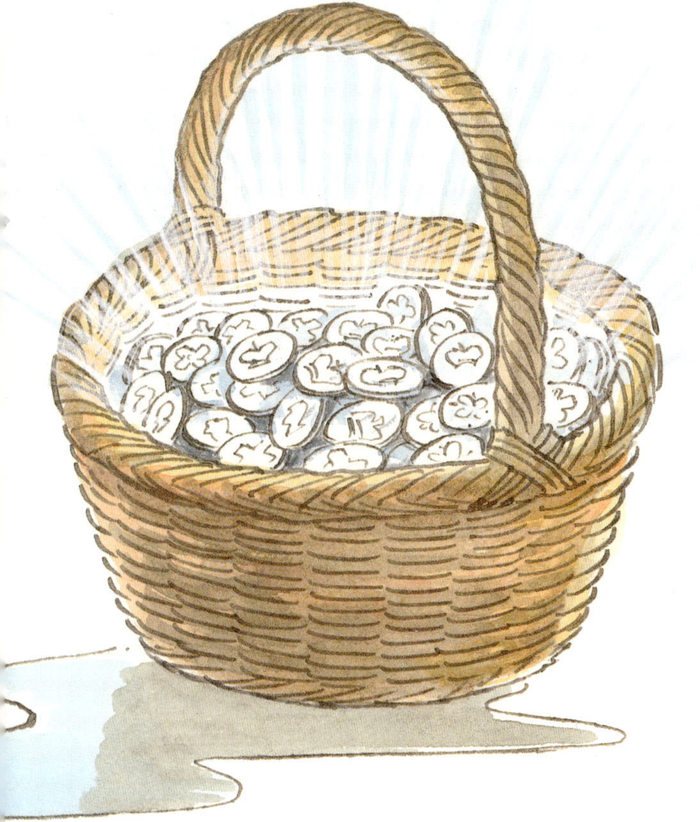

MY ROUND-THE-WORLD LIBRARY

First Edition Copyright © 1987
The Reader's Digest Association Limited,
Berkeley Square House, Berkeley Square,
London W1X 6AB

Reprinted 1990

Copyright © 1987
The Reader's Digest Association
Far East Limited

All rights reserved

® READER'S DIGEST, THE DIGEST and
the Pegasus logo are registered trademarks of
The Reader's Digest Association, Inc.
of Pleasantville, New York, U.S.A.

Printed in Hong Kong